LISTENING POINTER FOR THE TOEIC® TEST

基礎力アップ TOEIC® テスト リスニング

Osamu Yamaguchi
Tim Guire

SEIBIDO

音声ファイルのダウンロード／ストリーミング

CDマーク表示がある箇所は、音声を弊社HPより無料でダウンロード／ストリーミングすることができます。トップページのバナーをクリックし、書籍検索してください。書籍詳細ページに音声ダウンロードアイコンがございますのでそちらから自習用音声としてご活用ください。

https://www.seibido.co.jp

Listening Pointer for the TOEIC® Test

Copyright © 2003 by Osamu Yamaguchi, Tim Guire

All rights reserved for Japan
No part of this book may be reproduced in any form
without permission from Seibido Co., Ltd.

はしがき

　TOEICテストの重要性が益々高まっています。毎年数多くのTOEIC関連の出版物が世に出ていることが、このことを如実に物語っています。そして、質が高く、スコアアップのための実力が確実につく「真のTOEIC対策本」が、これまで以上に求められるようになってきています。

　このことは、TOEIC対策の大学テキストにおいても例外ではありません。大学での教材としてのTOEIC本は、単なるTOEIC対策だけではなく、教育的に価値のあるものでなければなりません。

　本書は、TOEICのリスニング対策テキストとして、スコアアップを目標としているのは勿論のこと、それにとどまらず、語彙や文法の確認もしながら、トータルな視点から英語を学ぶという、いわば「本物志向」のTOEIC対策教本です。

　本書によって、TOEIC攻略の要である語彙と文法の基本を押さえつつ、リスニング対策の基礎が学べます。各章始めに、「考えさせる」という知的活動に焦点を当てた「Vocabulary Check」があります。また、章ごとに文法テーマを設定し、各章終わりに「Grammar Pointer」を設け、文法事項を簡単に整理しています。

　本書は、各章2ページで完結し、全パートの問題計10問で構成しています。「Vocabulary Check」はその問題に現れる重要語を扱っています。文法はPart ⅠとPart Ⅱを通して確認できるようになっています。Part Ⅲは設問パターン別、Part Ⅳはジャンル別で構成されています。全20章からなる本書の最後には、Practice Testがあり、実力の総チェックが可能です。

　本書は、数と質において理想的な問題を、語彙と文法を確認しながら、TOEICスコアのUPと同時に「本物のコミュニケーション能力」の養成という、大学英語テキストとしての重要課題を達成できるように組合せ、教育上、効率と効果が最大になるという理念のもとに編まれています。

　本書を通じて、TOEICスコアの向上、更には、社会が求める「本物のコミュニケーション能力」の涵養に少しでも貢献すれば、望外の喜びです。

　最後に、本書の成立にお力添えをいただいた成美堂社長の佐野英一郎氏、および、編集の立場から色々と助言をいただいた編集部の木村臨氏に、心からの謝意を表明したいと思います。

2002年9月

著　者

本書の構成と利用法

本書は各Partごとに、次のようなテーマが設定されています。最後にPractice Test（ハーフテスト）があります。巻末に解答用紙がつけてあり、章ごとに切り離すことができます。各章の問題自体も切り離すことができますので、授業でうまく活用してください。

	Part I & II	Part III	Part IV
Chapter 1	進行形	会話の場所を問う	自己紹介スピーチ
Chapter 2	完了形	話者の職業を問う	ニュース報道
Chapter 3	受動態	話者の人間関係を問う	天気予報
Chapter 4	現在形	話者の現在の行動を問う	交通情報
Chapter 5	過去形	話者の過去の行動を問う	ビジネスレポート
Chapter 6	未来形	話者の未来の行動を問う	会議の案内スピーチ
Chapter 7	不定詞	何が起こるかを問う	講演者紹介スピーチ
Chapter 8	動名詞	話題を問う	専門的な講演
Chapter 9	分詞	話者の提案を問う	授業の冒頭部分
Chapter 10	前置詞	話者の意図を問う	イベント案内
Chapter 11	副詞	Whatの質問	商品の宣伝
Chapter 12	形容詞	Whoの質問	空港でのアナウンス
Chapter 13	名詞	Whichの質問	デパートでのアナウンス
Chapter 14	代名詞	Whenの質問	探し物のメッセージ
Chapter 15	自動詞	Whereの質問	呼び出しのアナウンス
Chapter 16	他動詞	Whyの質問	電話のメッセージ
Chapter 17	助動詞	Howの質問	観光案内
Chapter 18	仮定法	How muchの質問	図書館の利用案内
Chapter 19	接続詞	How oftenの質問	求人広告
Chapter 20	関係詞	How longの質問	式典での挨拶

各章の最初のVocabulary Checkは、学生の学習意欲を高めるために、クイズ的な方式を取っており、単に辞書で調べると言う単純作業ではなく「考えさせる」ことを要求しています。学生のレベルに応じ、教授資料にあるヒントを与えてください。次の4種類の問題形式が、章を通して繰り返されています。

Definition： 　単語について、その定義を選ぶ。
Completion： 　単語の定義を参考に、その単語の綴りの欠けている部分を補う。
Arrangement： 　文字を並べ替えて、英文の空所に当てはまる単語を作る。
Matching： 　単語の定義や使い方のヒントを参考に、その単語を選ぶ。

Contents

はしがき

本書の構成と利用法

CHAPTER 1 　　Progressive（進行形）
CHAPTER 2 　　Perfect（完了形）
CHAPTER 3 　　Passive（受動態）
CHAPTER 4 　　Present（現在形）
CHAPTER 5 　　Past（過去形）
CHAPTER 6 　　Future（未来形）
CHAPTER 7 　　Infinitive（不定詞）
CHAPTER 8 　　Gerunds（動名詞）
CHAPTER 9 　　Participles（分詞）
CHAPTER 10 　　Prepositions（前置詞）
CHAPTER 11 　　Adverbs（副詞）
CHAPTER 12 　　Adjectives（形容詞）
CHAPTER 13 　　Nouns（名詞）
CHAPTER 14 　　Pronouns（代名詞）
CHAPTER 15 　　Intransitive Verbs（自動詞）
CHAPTER 16 　　Transitive Verbs（他動詞）
CHAPTER 17 　　Auxiliary Verbs（助動詞）
CHAPTER 18 　　Subjunctive（仮定法）
CHAPTER 19 　　Conjunctions（接続詞）
CHAPTER 20 　　Relative Clauses（関係詞）

TOEIC® PRACTICE TEST

CHAPTER 1 進行形

◎ VOCABULARY CHECK ◎
Definition

(1) dustpan ・　　・(a) a person whose job involves traveling in a spacecraft
(2) destination ・　　・(b) a system of keeping money at the bank
(3) account ・　　・(c) a short-handled pan for swept-up refuse
(4) grillroom ・　　・(d) a meat-serving place which belongs to a hotel, etc.
(5) astronaut ・　　・(e) a place to which somebody is going or something is being sent

▶ PART I 1-01

1. Ⓐ Ⓑ Ⓒ Ⓓ

2. Ⓐ Ⓑ Ⓒ Ⓓ

▶ PART II 1-02

3. Mark your answer on your answer sheet.　　Ⓐ Ⓑ Ⓒ
4. Mark your answer on your answer sheet.　　Ⓐ Ⓑ Ⓒ
5. Mark your answer on your answer sheet.　　Ⓐ Ⓑ Ⓒ
6. Mark your answer on your answer sheet.　　Ⓐ Ⓑ Ⓒ

PART III 🎧 1-03

7. Where is this conversation taking place?
   (A) At a butcher's.
   (B) At a newsstand.
   (C) In a grillroom.
   (D) In a fast-food shop.

8. Where does this conversation mostly likely occur?
   (A) At a laundry.
   (B) At a bank.
   (C) At an insurance company.
   (D) At a lunch counter.

PART IV 🎧 1-04

9. How often does the man play basketball in a week?
   (A) Once a week.
   (B) Twice a week.
   (C) About 10 times a month.
   (D) Every day.

10. What does he probably want to do in the near future?
    (A) To enjoy space travel.
    (B) To study about heavenly bodies.
    (C) To get a Nobel Prize in physics.
    (D) To become a professional basketball player.

GRAMMAR POINTER 1　Progressive（進行形）

① 普通の進行形　→　be ＋ V-ing（～している、～しつつある）
② 進行形の受身　→　be ＋ being ＋ V-ed（～されつつある）
③ 完了の進行形　→　have ＋ been ＋ V-ing（ずっと～している）

例①　I am studying physics now.（私は今物理学を勉強しているところです）
例②　The computer is being repaired.（そのコンピュータは修理中です）
例③　I have been watching TV for 3 hours.（テレビを見て3時間になります）

CHAPTER 1

Class　　　No.　　　Name　　　Score ／10

CHAPTER 2 完了形

◎ VOCABULARY CHECK ◎
Completion
- (1) pie_   (a structure that provides access to vessels)
- (2) fi_m   (a business partnership of two or more persons)
- (3) _a_d   (set down on the ground after traveling by water or air)
- (4) _e_ha_i_   (a person skilled in repairing or using machines or tools)
- (5) i_eb_r_   (a mass of floating ice broken away from a glacier)

PART I　1-05

1.　Ⓐ Ⓑ Ⓒ Ⓓ　　2.　Ⓐ Ⓑ Ⓒ Ⓓ

PART II　1-06

3. Mark your answer on your answer sheet.　Ⓐ Ⓑ Ⓒ
4. Mark your answer on your answer sheet.　Ⓐ Ⓑ Ⓒ
5. Mark your answer on your answer sheet.　Ⓐ Ⓑ Ⓒ
6. Mark your answer on your answer sheet.　Ⓐ Ⓑ Ⓒ

PART III 🎧 1-07

7. Who is the man most likely to be?
   (A) Mechanic.
   (B) Salesman.
   (C) Teacher.
   (D) Icebreaker.

8. Who is the woman most likely to be?
   (A) Travel Agent.
   (B) Landlady.
   (C) Flight Attendant.
   (D) Immigration Officer

PART IV 🎧 1-08

9. What is the size of the iceberg A-1?
   (A) Bigger than New York State.
   (B) Smaller than New York State.
   (C) As big as Antarctica.
   (D) As big as New York State.

10. What are scientists concerned about in the Antarctic region?
    (A) It is getting bigger.
    (B) It is getting warmer.
    (C) It is getting colder.
    (D) It is getting smaller.

GRAMMAR POINTER 2 Perfect（完了形）

① 現在完了形 → have ＋ V-ed（完了と経験と継続の意味3つ）
② 過去完了形 → had ＋ V-ed
③ 未来完了形 → will have ＋ V-ed

例① She has visited Paris before.（彼女は以前パリを訪れたことがある）
例② He said he had slept for 10 hours.（彼は10時間も寝てしまったと言った）
例③ I will have worked for 20 years next year.（来年勤続20年になる）

CHAPTER 2

Class　　　No.　　　Name　　　Score ／10

CHAPTER 3 受動態

◎ VOCABULARY CHECK ◎
Arrangement

(1) We (　　　　) our hands in front of a Shinto shrine.　　[pacl]
(2) The sheep were feeding in the fertile (　　　　).　　[doamew]
(3) They really wanted to (　　　　) in the athletic meet.　　[aaeiicpprtt]
(4) He (　　　　) up with the gas at a nearby gas station.　　[liefld]
(5) The weather (　　　　) said the sky would clear up.　　[recatsorfe]

PART I　1-09

1.　Ⓐ Ⓑ Ⓒ Ⓓ　　2.　Ⓐ Ⓑ Ⓒ Ⓓ

PART II　1-10

3. Mark your answer on your answer sheet.　　Ⓐ Ⓑ Ⓒ
4. Mark your answer on your answer sheet.　　Ⓐ Ⓑ Ⓒ
5. Mark your answer on your answer sheet.　　Ⓐ Ⓑ Ⓒ
6. Mark your answer on your answer sheet.　　Ⓐ Ⓑ Ⓒ

PART III 🎧 1-11

7. How do the man and woman know each other?
   (A) They are best friends.
   (B) They are co-workers.
   (C) They are homemakers.
   (D) They are classmates.

8. What is the relationship between the man and the woman?
   (A) Child and his mother.
   (B) Father and his daughter.
   (C) Engineer and his boss.
   (D) Salesman and his customer.

PART IV 🎧 1-12

9. What does the forecaster say about the weather on Wednesday and Thursday?
   (A) It will be hot and humid.
   (B) It will be cloudy and cooler.
   (C) It will be rainy.
   (D) It will be the same as today's weather.

10. When does the forecaster say it will rain?
    (A) Monday and Tuesday.
    (B) Friday and Saturday.
    (C) Sunday.
    (D) Monday through Friday.

GRAMMAR POINTER 3　Passive（受動態）

① 現在の受動態　→　am/are/is ＋ V-ed（〜される、〜されている）
② 過去の受動態　→　was/were ＋ V-ed（〜された、〜されていた）
③ 未来の受動態　→　will be ＋ V-ed（〜されるだろう）

例① Mt. Fuji is covered with snow.（富士山は雪で覆われている）
例② I was asked what I had eaten.（私は何を食べたか尋ねられた）
例③ The child will be taken to a park.（その子は公園へ連れて行かれるだろう）

CHAPTER 3

Class　　　No.　　　Name　　　Score ／10

CHAPTER 4 現在形

◎ **VOCABULARY CHECK** ◎
Matching

(1) I would like to make a (　　　　) for flight 506　・　　・ (a) vest
　　on Tuesday.
(2) a sleeveless garment worn over a shirt and under a jacket　・　　・ (b) piled
(3) His car (　　　　) through the jammed traffic.　・　　・ (c) reservation
(4) a person who provides emergency medical treatment　・　　・ (d) crawled
(5) The ship is (　　　　) up with containers.　・　　・ (e) paramedic
　　=Containers are (　　　　) up on the ship.

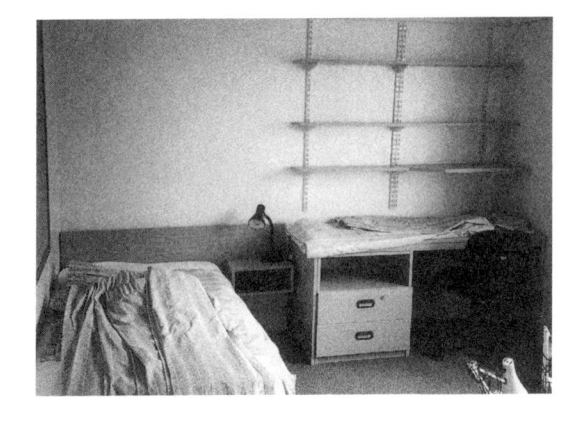

PART I　1-13

1.　Ⓐ Ⓑ Ⓒ Ⓓ　　2.　Ⓐ Ⓑ Ⓒ Ⓓ

PART II　1-14

3. Mark your answer on your answer sheet.　Ⓐ Ⓑ Ⓒ
4. Mark your answer on your answer sheet.　Ⓐ Ⓑ Ⓒ
5. Mark your answer on your answer sheet.　Ⓐ Ⓑ Ⓒ
6. Mark your answer on your answer sheet.　Ⓐ Ⓑ Ⓒ

PART III 🎧 1-15

7. What is the woman doing?
   (A) Making airline reservations.
   (B) Writing about travel.
   (C) Reading a book.
   (D) Arguing with the man.

8. What is John doing?
   (A) Sleeping.
   (B) Calling.
   (C) Studying.
   (D) Exercising.

PART IV 🎧 1-16

9. What is slowing traffic down on the north side of town?
   (A) A car accident.
   (B) Construction work.
   (C) Rush hour.
   (D) Police.

10. How many cars were there in the car accident?
    (A) 1
    (B) 2
    (C) 3
    (D) 4

GRAMMAR POINTER 4　　Present（現在形）

　　① 現在の状態を表す　→　状態動詞が用いられる（～している）
　　② 現在の習慣を表す　→　動作動詞が用いられる（～する、～している）
　　③ 近未来の予定を表す　→　往来発着系動詞が用いられる（～する）

例① I know that he is a doctor.（私は彼が医者であることを知っている）
例② She works every other day.（彼女は一日おきに働いている）
例③ His train leaves at 7 o'clock.（彼の列車は7時に出発する）

CHAPTER 4

Class　　　　　　No.　　　　　　Name　　　　　　Score　　／10

CHAPTER 5 過去形

◎ **VOCABULARY CHECK** ◎
Definition

(1) strike　　・　　・(a) announce by a public notice
(2) commence ・　　・(b) belonging exclusively to one person or group
(3) peculiar　 ・　　・(c) indicate the hour by a sound
(4) inventory ・　　・(d) start to do something
(5) post　　　・　　・(e) the process of making a list of goods in stock

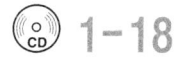

PART I　1-17

1.　Ⓐ Ⓑ Ⓒ Ⓓ　　2.　Ⓐ Ⓑ Ⓒ Ⓓ

PART II　1-18

3. Mark your answer on your answer sheet.　Ⓐ Ⓑ Ⓒ
4. Mark your answer on your answer sheet.　Ⓐ Ⓑ Ⓒ
5. Mark your answer on your answer sheet.　Ⓐ Ⓑ Ⓒ
6. Mark your answer on your answer sheet.　Ⓐ Ⓑ Ⓒ

PART III 🎧 1-19

7. What happened to the man?
   (A) He had a rotten orange.
   (B) He found her an apple polisher.
   (C) He ate a bad piece of fruit.
   (D) He saw some peculiar fruit.

8. What did the woman do?
   (A) She went to an interview.
   (B) She started work at her new job.
   (C) She went to her job.
   (D) She quit the company.

PART IV 🎧 1-20

9. What position is Alpha Books Incorporated currently ranked?
   (A) First position.
   (B) Second position.
   (C) Third position.
   (D) Fourth position.

10. What is a factor which improved Alpha Books Incorporated's performance?
    (A) Lower sales.
    (B) Communications satellites.
    (C) Inventory management.
    (D) 10% downsizing of the staff.

GRAMMAR POINTER 5　Past（過去形）

① 過去の状態を表す　→　状態動詞が用いられる（～していた）
② 過去の動作を表す　→　動作動詞が用いられる（～した）
③ 過去の習慣を表す　→　used to do が用いられる（～したものだ）

例① My friend belonged to a choir.（私の友人は聖歌隊に属していた）
例② He studied for five hours yesterday.（彼は昨日 5 時間勉強した）
例③ I used to take a walk every morning.（私は毎朝散歩をしたものだ）

CHAPTER 5

Class　　　　　No.　　　　　Name　　　　　Score ／10

CHAPTER 6 未来形

◎ **VOCABULARY CHECK** ◎
Completion
(1) sky_c_a_e_ (an extremely tall building)
(2) appl_ca_i_n (a form used to make a request for employment, etc.)
(3) _o_p_e_e (finish doing something or bring it to an end)
(4) b_o_in_ (rapidly growing or developing)
(5) i_b_l_n_e (a situation in which two or more things are not the same size)

PART I 1-21

1. Ⓐ Ⓑ Ⓒ Ⓓ
2. Ⓐ Ⓑ Ⓒ Ⓓ

PART II 1-22

3. Mark your answer on your answer sheet.   Ⓐ Ⓑ Ⓒ
4. Mark your answer on your answer sheet.   Ⓐ Ⓑ Ⓒ
5. Mark your answer on your answer sheet.   Ⓐ Ⓑ Ⓒ
6. Mark your answer on your answer sheet.   Ⓐ Ⓑ Ⓒ

PART III CD 1-23

7. What is the man trying to do?
   (A) Make a bet.
   (B) Complete his work.
   (C) Stay for dinner.
   (D) Drink wine late.

8. What will the woman do?
   (A) Work on the computer.
   (B) Go to work.
   (C) Return the computer.
   (D) Take over the work.

PART IV CD 1-24

9. What is the subject of the conference?
   (A) European politics.
   (B) Asian economies.
   (C) Trade imbalance.
   (D) Booming foundations.

10. What kind of effort is needed to revive the former booming economies?
    (A) Individual.
    (B) Relaxed.
    (C) Combined.
    (D) Grass-roots.

GRAMMAR POINTER 6　Future（未来形）

① 未来の事象を表す　→　will do（単純未来と意志未来の2つ）
② 未来の予定を表す　→　be going to do を用いる（～する予定だ）
③ 極めて近い未来を表す　→　be about to do を用いる（～するところだ）

例① It will probably rain soon, so I will not go.（雨が降りそうだから行かないよ）
例② I am going to travel around the world.（私は世界一周旅行を予定している）
例③ Something happy is about to happen.（何か楽しいことが起こりそうだ）

CHAPTER 6

Class　　　No.　　　Name　　　Score　/10

CHAPTER 7 不定詞

◎ **VOCABULARY CHECK** ◎

Arrangement

(1) A variety of (　　　　　) machines are found in a city.　　　[gnidnev]
(2) The chemist made many experiments in his (　　　　　).　　[aaooytrlbr]
(3) The story (　　　　　) her of her happy school days.　　　[derimnde]
(4) Let's give a round of (　　　　　) to our guest speaker.　　[saleupap]
(5) My secretary will (　　　　　) you of your client's arrival.　[rofmin]

PART I　　1-25

1.　Ⓐ Ⓑ Ⓒ Ⓓ　　　　2.　Ⓐ Ⓑ Ⓒ Ⓓ

PART II　　1-26

3. Mark your answer on your answer sheet.　　Ⓐ Ⓑ Ⓒ
4. Mark your answer on your answer sheet.　　Ⓐ Ⓑ Ⓒ
5. Mark your answer on your answer sheet.　　Ⓐ Ⓑ Ⓒ
6. Mark your answer on your answer sheet.　　Ⓐ Ⓑ Ⓒ

PART III 🎧 1-27

7. What will probably happen?
   (A) The man will be on time.
   (B) The man will make it.
   (C) The man will feel good.
   (D) The man will be late.

8. What will probably happen?
   (A) The man will call Mr. Jones.
   (B) The woman will call on Mr. Jones.
   (C) Mr. Jones will telephone the woman later.
   (D) The woman will see Mr. Jones this afternoon.

PART IV 🎧 1-28

9. What is the woman's former occupation?
   (A) A psychologist.
   (B) A professor of international relations.
   (C) A business consultant.
   (D) A section chief of a company.

10. Why is the woman known to the audience?
    (A) Because she is often on TV.
    (B) Because her book sold well.
    (C) Because she gave several lectures to the audience before.
    (D) Because they were already informed about her in their employee magazine.

GRAMMAR POINTER 7　Infinitive (不定詞)

① 名詞的用法　→　to do...（...すること）
② 形容詞的用法　→　N to do...（...するためのN）
③ 副詞的用法　→　V～to do...（...するためにV～する）

例①　It is important to study English.（英語を勉強することが重要である）
例②　I want something to drink.（飲むための何か [=何か飲み物] が欲しい）
例③　She went to the shop to buy it.（彼女はそれを買うためにその店に行った）

CHAPTER 7

Class　　　　No.　　　　Name　　　　Score　　／10

CHAPTER 8 動名詞

◎ **VOCABULARY CHECK** ◎

Matching

(1) very unhappy or uncomfortable · · (a) purpose
(2) Religious miracles are beyond the (   ) · · (b) fault
    of human knowledge.
(3) for the (   ) of doing...= in order to do... · · (c) boundary
(4) a person who specializes in removing dirt from clothes · · (d) miserable
(5) a relatively long crack in the hard surface layer of · · (e) cleaner
    the earth

PART I 1-29

1. Ⓐ Ⓑ Ⓒ Ⓓ

2. Ⓐ Ⓑ Ⓒ Ⓓ

PART II 1-30

3. Mark your answer on your answer sheet.   Ⓐ Ⓑ Ⓒ
4. Mark your answer on your answer sheet.   Ⓐ Ⓑ Ⓒ
5. Mark your answer on your answer sheet.   Ⓐ Ⓑ Ⓒ
6. Mark your answer on your answer sheet.   Ⓐ Ⓑ Ⓒ

PART III 🎧 1-31

7. What is the topic of their discussion?
   (A) Four casts.
   (B) A heavy rain.
   (C) The weather.
   (D) A miserable meal.

8. What are they discussing?
   (A) Salary.
   (B) Expenses.
   (C) Food.
   (D) Dolls.

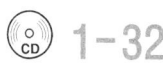

PART IV 🎧 1-32

9. What is the topic of this lecture?
   (A) Hurricanes.
   (B) Tornadoes.
   (C) Earthquakes.
   (D) Volcanoes.

10. How many kinds of plate boundaries are there?
    (A) 1
    (B) 2
    (C) 3
    (D) 4

GRAMMAR POINTER 8　Gerunds (動名詞)

① 動名詞の基本形　→　doing... (...すること)
② 動名詞の完了形　→　having done... (...したこと)
③ 動名詞の否定形　→　not doing... (...しないこと)

例①　Seeing is believing.（見ることは信じることだ [=百聞は一見に如かず]）
例②　She felt regret for having done it.（彼女はそれをしたことを後悔した）
例③　He insists on not going there.（彼はそこには行かないと言い張っている）

CHAPTER 8

Class　　　No.　　　Name　　　Score　／10

CHAPTER 9 分詞

◎ VOCABULARY CHECK ◎
Definition

(1) line · · (a) mail sent electronically through the computer
(2) e-mail · · (b) make something invalid or decide not to do it
(3) cancel · · (c) be arranged in such a way that it forms a row
(4) doctorate · · (d) scheduled or expected to do something
(5) due · · (e) the degree, status or title of an academic doctor

PART I 1-33

1. Ⓐ Ⓑ Ⓒ Ⓓ

2. Ⓐ Ⓑ Ⓒ Ⓓ

PART II 1-34

3. Mark your answer on your answer sheet.   Ⓐ Ⓑ Ⓒ
4. Mark your answer on your answer sheet.   Ⓐ Ⓑ Ⓒ
5. Mark your answer on your answer sheet.   Ⓐ Ⓑ Ⓒ
6. Mark your answer on your answer sheet.   Ⓐ Ⓑ Ⓒ

PART III 💿 1-35

7. What does the man suggest?
   (A) Staying with her job.
   (B) Searching for another job.
   (C) Doing a better job.
   (D) Getting a different friend.

8. What does the woman suggest?
   (A) Renting a movie.
   (B) Finishing the report.
   (C) Watching a film.
   (D) Going to school.

PART IV 💿 1-36

9. What type of class is this sociology class?
   (A) Introductory.
   (B) Intermediate.
   (C) Masters level.
   (D) Doctorate level.

10. What does the lecturer expect from the students?
    (A) A term paper.
    (B) Social behavior.
    (C) A good group.
    (D) Attendance.

GRAMMAR POINTER 9　Participles（分詞）

① 分詞の基本用法　→　be＋現在分詞 / be＋過去分詞 / have＋過去分詞
② 分詞の形容詞的用法　→　N＋doing / done...（...している/されるN）
③ 分詞の副詞的用法　→　V～doing / done...（...して/されてV～する）

例①　The house has been being built.（その家は建てられつつある状態だ）
例②　The child sleeping in bed is hers.（ベッドで眠っている子は彼女の子だ）
例③　She sat on the chair knitting.（彼女は編物をしながら椅子に座っていた）

CHAPTER 9

Class _____　No. _____　Name _____　Score ___／10

CHAPTER 10 前置詞

◎ VOCABULARY CHECK ◎
Completion

(1) _h_to_o_ie_ (a machine which reproduces printed matter)
(2) g_f_w_a_ (specially package something with paper as a gift)
(3) _a_d_a_e (metal ware as machine parts, tools and utensils)
(4) _w_r_ (give a prize in praise of good quality or performance)
(5) _e_i_t_a_io_ (the act of enrolling a thing or person formally)

PART I　1-37

1.　Ⓐ Ⓑ Ⓒ Ⓓ　　2.　Ⓐ Ⓑ Ⓒ Ⓓ

PART II　1-38

3. Mark your answer on your answer sheet.　Ⓐ Ⓑ Ⓒ
4. Mark your answer on your answer sheet.　Ⓐ Ⓑ Ⓒ
5. Mark your answer on your answer sheet.　Ⓐ Ⓑ Ⓒ
6. Mark your answer on your answer sheet.　Ⓐ Ⓑ Ⓒ

PART III CD 1-39

7. What does the man intend to do?
   (A) Relax all summer long.
   (B) Go swimming.
   (C) Plan a store.
   (D) Get a job.

8. What does the woman intend to do?
   (A) Finish the report today.
   (B) Complete the assignment tomorrow.
   (C) Go fishing.
   (D) Listen to the report.

PART IV CD 1-40

9. How often does the chess club have its chess championship event?
   (A) Twice a month.
   (B) Twice a year.
   (C) Once a month.
   (D) Once a year.

10. Where can registration forms be found?
    (A) At the high school.
    (B) At convenience stores.
    (C) In the mailbox.
    (D) In the classroom.

GRAMMAR POINTER 10 Prepositions（前置詞）

① N＋前置詞句 → 前置詞句は形容詞的用法でNを修飾する
② A＋前置詞句 → 前置詞句は副詞的用法でAを修飾する
③ V〜＋前置詞句 → 前置詞句は副詞的用法でV〜を修飾する

例① I have a keen interest in physics.（私は物理学に大変興味がある）
例② He is afraid of making mistakes.（彼は過ちを犯すことを恐れている）
例③ Will you listen carefully to the report?（報告を注意して聞いて下さい）

CHAPTER 10

Class _____ No. _____ Name _____ Score ___/10

CHAPTER 11 副詞

◎ **VOCABULARY CHECK** ◎
Arrangement

(1) The police officer put (　　　　　) on the thief.　　　　[sfundcafh]

(2) The signboard reads, "All drinks are to be drunk on the
    (　　　　　)."　　　　　　　　　　　　　　　　　　　[eimpress]

(3) Did you (　　　　　) the rumor that he had been fired?　　[haverero]

(4) (　　　　　) include not only jewelry but also hats or bags.
    　　　　　　　　　　　　　　　　　　　　　　　　[ccrsssaeeio]

(5) I was asked how much the parcel (　　　　　) by the post office
    supervisor.　　　　　　　　　　　　　　　　　　　　　[higewde]

PART I　　2-01

1.　Ⓐ Ⓑ Ⓒ Ⓓ

2.　Ⓐ Ⓑ Ⓒ Ⓓ

PART II　　2-02

3. Mark your answer on your answer sheet.　Ⓐ Ⓑ Ⓒ
4. Mark your answer on your answer sheet.　Ⓐ Ⓑ Ⓒ
5. Mark your answer on your answer sheet.　Ⓐ Ⓑ Ⓒ
6. Mark your answer on your answer sheet.　Ⓐ Ⓑ Ⓒ

PART III 2-03

7. What does the man say about John?
   (A) John is very busy.
   (B) He will speak to John.
   (C) John is not needed for the job.
   (D) He has seen John at work.

8. What did the woman buy?
   (A) Clothes.
   (B) Luggage.
   (C) Accessories.
   (D) A ring.

PART IV 2-04

9. What is the XL Super Camera being called?
   (A) The Best in Home Protection.
   (B) The Most Affordable Camera.
   (C) The Improved XL Camera.
   (D) The Future of Home Protection.

10. How much does the mini-XL Super Camera cost?
    (A) $115.
    (B) $150.
    (C) $250.
    (D) $275.

GRAMMAR POINTER 11　Adverbs（副詞）

① 様態を表す副詞　→　V〜（動詞句）の直後にくる　[quickly, kindly等]
② 頻度を表す副詞　→　V（一般動詞）の直前にくる　[often, always等]
③ 文副詞　→　主に文頭にくる [honestly, surprisingly, probably等]

例① He eats lunch quickly in most cases.（彼は大抵、昼食を急いで食べる）
例② She often plays the piano in fall.（彼女は秋にはよくピアノを弾く）
例③ Surprisingly, he performed miracles.（驚いたことに彼は奇跡を起こした）

CHAPTER 11

Class　　　No.　　　Name　　　Score　／10

CHAPTER 12 形容詞

◎ **VOCABULARY CHECK** ◎
Matching
(1) to hang or bend downward　　　　　　　　　・　　・(a) shaded
(2) A local hospital was (　　　　　) for use in　・　　・(b) grade
　　an emergency.
(3) "(　　　　　) students" usually means those　・　　・(c) designated
　　coming from abroad.
(4) She (　　　　　) the drawing of the grape to　・　　・(d) overseas
　　make it more natural.
(5) The student got a (　　　　　) of seventy-two　・　　・(e) droop
　　on the test.

PART I　2-05

1. Ⓐ Ⓑ Ⓒ Ⓓ

2. Ⓐ Ⓑ Ⓒ Ⓓ

PART II　2-06

3. Mark your answer on your answer sheet.　Ⓐ Ⓑ Ⓒ
4. Mark your answer on your answer sheet.　Ⓐ Ⓑ Ⓒ
5. Mark your answer on your answer sheet.　Ⓐ Ⓑ Ⓒ
6. Mark your answer on your answer sheet.　Ⓐ Ⓑ Ⓒ

PART III 2-07

7. Who is the man talking with?
   (A) The babysitter.
   (B) His kids.
   (C) His grandfather.
   (D) His wife.

8. Who did the woman meet?
   (A) A teacher.
   (B) A friend.
   (C) A doctor.
   (D) A student.

PART IV 2-08

9. What type of car is parked in a no-parking zone?
   (A) A red pickup truck.
   (B) A blue airport limousine.
   (C) Red Toyota Lexus.
   (D) Blue Toyota Corolla.

10. Which areas are designated as pick-up and drop-off areas?
    (A) Areas shaded blue.
    (B) Areas shaded yellow.
    (C) Areas shaded red.
    (D) Areas shaded violet.

GRAMMAR POINTER 12　Adjectives（形容詞）

① 叙述用法　→　SVCやSVOCのC（補語＝文の要素）になる
② 限定用法　→　＜A＋N＞におけるA（修飾語＝語の付加要素）になる
③ 主観的意見のA（useful等）が客観的情報のA（wooden等）の前にくる

例①　I found the boy brave.（私はその少年が勇敢であることに気づいた）
例②　She is a pretty intelligent girl.（彼女はかなり頭のよい少女だ）
例③　This is a useful big old wooden box.（これは役に立つ大きな古い木箱だ）

CHAPTER 12

Class　　　　　No.　　　　　Name　　　　　Score　／10

CHAPTER 13 名詞

◎ VOCABULARY CHECK ◎
Definition

(1) hoist · · (a) easy to use, learn or deal with
(2) microscope · · (b) subtract a certain sum of money from a fixed price
(3) user-friendly · · (c) raise or haul up an object like a flag
(4) algebra · · (d) an instrument used to see very small objects
(5) discount · · (e) a branch of mathematics in which symbols represent quantities

PART I 2-09

1. Ⓐ Ⓑ Ⓒ Ⓓ
2. Ⓐ Ⓑ Ⓒ Ⓓ

PART II 2-10

3. Mark your answer on your answer sheet. Ⓐ Ⓑ Ⓒ
4. Mark your answer on your answer sheet. Ⓐ Ⓑ Ⓒ
5. Mark your answer on your answer sheet. Ⓐ Ⓑ Ⓒ
6. Mark your answer on your answer sheet. Ⓐ Ⓑ Ⓒ

PART III 2-11

7. Which type of test was the most difficult?
   (A) The English test.
   (B) The science test.
   (C) The math test.
   (D) The history test.

8. Which type of car does the woman want?
   (A) The modern red car.
   (B) The old red car.
   (C) The brand car.
   (D) The new yellow car.

PART IV 2-12

9. How long is the sale?
   (A) 5 minutes.
   (B) 15 minutes.
   (C) 30 minutes.
   (D) 50 minutes.

10. Which department is having a sale?
    (A) Women's Department.
    (B) Shoe Department.
    (C) Men's Department.
    (D) Household Goods Department.

GRAMMAR POINTER 13   Nouns（名詞）

① 可算名詞 → 主に普通名詞でa N, the N, N-s, the N-sの4つの形
② 不可算名詞 → 主に物質名詞や抽象名詞でN, the Nの2つの形
③ 物質名詞や抽象名詞も数えることがある

例① He is a poet and novelist.（彼は詩人兼小説家だ）［冠詞省略は同一人物］
例② There is some wine left in the bottle.（ボトルに少しワインが残っている）
例③ I like French wines.（私はフランス産のワイン類が好きだ）［×...wine.］

CHAPTER 13

Class　　　　　No.　　　　　Name　　　　　Score　／10

CHAPTER 14 代名詞

◎ **VOCABULARY CHECK** ◎
Completion
(1) _a_a_e_e_t   [the practice of controlling a business or its staff]
(2) bu_ld   [the physical form of a thing or person]
(3) c_nv_r_ib_e   [a car with a top that can be folded back or removed]
(4) l_f_sa_e_   [a person who provides help in a crisis or emergency]
(5) diam_n_   [a playing field for baseball]

PART I 2-13

1. Ⓐ Ⓑ Ⓒ Ⓓ
2. Ⓐ Ⓑ Ⓒ Ⓓ

PART II 2-14

3. Mark your answer on your answer sheet.   Ⓐ Ⓑ Ⓒ
4. Mark your answer on your answer sheet.   Ⓐ Ⓑ Ⓒ
5. Mark your answer on your answer sheet.   Ⓐ Ⓑ Ⓒ
6. Mark your answer on your answer sheet.   Ⓐ Ⓑ Ⓒ

PART III 💿 2-15

7. When did the man mail the letter?
   (A) Yesterday.
   (B) Last week.
   (C) Four days ago.
   (D) Two days ago.

8. When will the next race take place?
   (A) Spring.
   (B) Summer.
   (C) In one year.
   (D) In two weeks.

PART IV 💿 2-16

9. What kind of dog is Calvin?
   (A) Collie.
   (B) German sheperd.
   (C) Golden retriever.
   (D) Greyhound.

10. Where was Calvin last seen?
    (A) Near his home.
    (B) Near the baseball diamond.
    (C) Near the basketball courts.
    (D) Near the river.

GRAMMAR POINTER 14　Pronouns（代名詞）

① 人称代名詞　→　1人称（I, we）と2人称（you）と3人称（he, she, it, they）
② 指示代名詞　→　「これ」（this / these）と「それ・あれ」（that / those）
③ 特別の代名詞　→　再帰代名詞（oneself）と相互代名詞（each other 等）

例①　Thinking makes what you read yours.（思考すれば読書がものになる）
例②　What are those things you are carrying?（あなたがお持ちのそれは何ですか）
例③　They looked at each other.（彼らはお互い見つめ合った）［at省略は不可］

CHAPTER 14

Class　　　　No.　　　　Name　　　　Score　／10

CHAPTER 15 自動詞

◎ **VOCABULARY CHECK** ◎
Arrangement
(1) "(   ) car" in English often means a "ropeway."   [lebac]
(2) It is better to take a (   ) umbrella with you today.   [palebillsoc]
(3) The IT-related business has not been (   ) recently.   [pingay]
(4) You should not copy the answers from your (   ).   [boringhe]
(5) He was asked to (   ) to the head office at 8 o'clock.   [toprer]

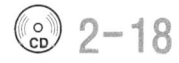

PART I   2-17

1. Ⓐ Ⓑ Ⓒ Ⓓ
2. Ⓐ Ⓑ Ⓒ Ⓓ

PART II   2-18

3. Mark your answer on your answer sheet.   Ⓐ Ⓑ Ⓒ
4. Mark your answer on your answer sheet.   Ⓐ Ⓑ Ⓒ
5. Mark your answer on your answer sheet.   Ⓐ Ⓑ Ⓒ
6. Mark your answer on your answer sheet.   Ⓐ Ⓑ Ⓒ

PART III 2-19

7. Where did the man find the ball?
   (A) In his garden.
   (B) In his neighbor's yard.
   (C) On the floor.
   (D) On the farm.

8. Where does the woman want to visit?
   (A) Europe.
   (B) Asia.
   (C) North America.
   (D) Oceania.

PART IV 2-20

9. How many Customer Service counters are there?
   (A) 1
   (B) 2
   (C) 3
   (D) 4

10. Why was Robert Jones paged?
    (A) To fill out a report.
    (B) To receive an item.
    (C) He had a phone call.
    (D) His lost cell phone was found.

GRAMMAR POINTER 15　Intransitive Verbs（自動詞）

① 他動詞で有名な動詞の自動詞用法　→　takeやpay等基本語に多い
② 受動態的意味を持つ自動詞用法　→　sellやplay等基本語に多い
③ その他注意すべき自動詞用法　→　writeの用法に注目

例①　She takes well.（写真写りがよい）/ Honesty does not pay.（正直は損する）
例②　The book sold well.（よく売れた）/ What will play next?（次の演奏は何？）
例③　He writes poorly.（文章が下手だ）/ This pen writes poorly.（書きにくい）

CHAPTER 15

Class　　　　No.　　　　Name　　　　Score　　/10

CHAPTER 16 他動詞

◎ **VOCABULARY CHECK** ◎

Matching

(1) The supplier (　　　　) to us for the delay　・　・ (a) apologized
　　of 10 days in their delivery of our order.

(2) (　　　　) a dog daily = take a dog for a　・　・ (b) board
　　(　　　　) every day

(3) get on a large vehicle like a ship, plane, train, or bus　・　・ (c) walk

(4) John often (　　　　)-parks when he is　・　・ (d) missed
　　in a hurry.

(5) I (　　　　) attending the party due to　・　・ (e) double
　　my carelessness.

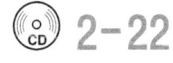

PART I　2-21

1. Ⓐ Ⓑ Ⓒ Ⓓ

2. Ⓐ Ⓑ Ⓒ Ⓓ

PART II　2-22

3. Mark your answer on your answer sheet.　Ⓐ Ⓑ Ⓒ
4. Mark your answer on your answer sheet.　Ⓐ Ⓑ Ⓒ
5. Mark your answer on your answer sheet.　Ⓐ Ⓑ Ⓒ
6. Mark your answer on your answer sheet.　Ⓐ Ⓑ Ⓒ

PART III 🎵 2-23

7. Why was the man late?
   (A) He failed to catch the bus.
   (B) He didn't take a taxi.
   (C) He missed the train.
   (D) He took the wrong bus.

8. Why did the woman fail the test?
   (A) She studied too long.
   (B) She was late for the test.
   (C) She did not study.
   (D) The test was too hard.

PART IV 🎵 2-24

9. How many books did Thomas Hart order?
   (A) 1
   (B) 2
   (C) 3
   (D) 4

10. Why did one book not arrive?
    (A) It was lost in the mail.
    (B) The company forgot to send it.
    (C) It was not ordered.
    (D) It was out of stock.

GRAMMAR POINTER 16 Transitive Verbs（他動詞）

① 自動詞で有名な動詞の他動詞用法 → walkやtalk等基本語に多い
② 自動詞と間違いやすい他動詞 → discussやmention等がある
③ 名詞で有名な単語の他動詞用法 → water等基本名詞に多い

例① I will walk you to the station.（駅まで歩いてお送りしましょう）
例② Let us discuss the issue.（その案件を議論しましょう）[×discuss about]
例③ She waters the flowers every morning.（彼女は毎朝その花に水をやる）

CHAPTER 16

Class　　　No.　　　Name　　　Score　／10

CHAPTER 17 助動詞

◎ VOCABULARY CHECK ◎
Definition

(1) corner ・　　・(a) being made lower in rank or position
(2) crash ・　　・(b) being raised to a higher rank or position
(3) promotion ・　　・(c) break noisily or make a sudden loud noise
(4) demotion ・　　・(d) the place where two surfaces or lines meet
(5) reef ・　　・(e) a ridge of sand, coral, etc. that rises to or close to the water surface

PART I   2-25

1. Ⓐ Ⓑ Ⓒ Ⓓ

2. Ⓐ Ⓑ Ⓒ Ⓓ

PART II   2-26

3. Mark your answer on your answer sheet.　　Ⓐ Ⓑ Ⓒ
4. Mark your answer on your answer sheet.　　Ⓐ Ⓑ Ⓒ
5. Mark your answer on your answer sheet.　　Ⓐ Ⓑ Ⓒ
6. Mark your answer on your answer sheet.　　Ⓐ Ⓑ Ⓒ

PART III 💿 2-27

7. How will the man go to work?
   (A) By train.
   (B) By bus.
   (C) On foot.
   (D) In his car.

8. How many cookies does the woman want?
   (A) 10.
   (B) 12.
   (C) 20.
   (D) 30.

PART IV 💿 2-28

9. What is the bay floor of Hanauma Bay?
   (A) The crater of a volcano.
   (B) Rocky ledges.
   (C) Sharp rocks.
   (D) Sand.

10. Why should people avoid walking on the reef?
    (A) It can become slippery.
    (B) It is unpredictable.
    (C) It is where waves break.
    (D) It is a live reef.

GRAMMAR POINTER 17　Auxiliary Verbs（助動詞）

① 助動詞の基本形　→　will, must, may, can が中心で、意味は2つずつ
② 助動詞の過去形　→　would, might, could, should で、意味は「丁寧」
③ 助動詞の特殊形　→　may have V-ed と must have V-ed が重要

例①　It will rain.（雨が降るだろう）/ I will go.（私は行くつもりです）
例②　Would you tell me about it?（それについて教えてくださいませんか）
例③　She may have gone shopping.（彼女は買い物に出かけたかもしれない）

CHAPTER 17

Class　　　　　No.　　　　　Name　　　　　Score / 10

CHAPTER 18 仮定法

◎ VOCABULARY CHECK ◎
Completion

(1) _o_p_a_n (express feelings of pain, anger or dissatisfaction)

(2) _pp_e_ia_e (feel gratitude for something, or recognize its value)

(3) i_l_s_ra_ed (provided with explanatory and decorative features)

(4) _u_f_c_e_t (as much as is needed or desired)

(5) _l_h_b_t_z_ (arrange items in the traditional order of letters)

PART I 2-29

1. Ⓐ Ⓑ Ⓒ Ⓓ

2. Ⓐ Ⓑ Ⓒ Ⓓ

PART II 2-30

3. Mark your answer on your answer sheet. Ⓐ Ⓑ Ⓒ

4. Mark your answer on your answer sheet. Ⓐ Ⓑ Ⓒ

5. Mark your answer on your answer sheet. Ⓐ Ⓑ Ⓒ

6. Mark your answer on your answer sheet. Ⓐ Ⓑ Ⓒ

PART III 2-31

7. How much time is left in the movie?
   (A) Around an hour.
   (B) Half an hour or so.
   (C) 13 minutes.
   (D) Only about 30 seconds.

8. How much wine is there?
   (A) A lot.
   (B) None.
   (C) A small amount.
   (D) A sufficient amount.

PART IV 2-32

9. What is needed to check books out?
   (A) Money.
   (B) Library pass.
   (C) Library card.
   (D) Subject card.

10. How are books alphabetized?
    (A) By author's first name.
    (B) By author's family name.
    (C) By subject.
    (D) By the title of a book.

GRAMMAR POINTER 18　Subjunctive（仮定法）

① 仮定法過去　→　S would V ~ if S' V'-ed ....
② 仮定法過去完了　→　S would have V-ed if S' had V'-ed ....
③ 仮定法should　→　S would V ~ if S' should V' ....

例①　I would fly to you if I were a bird.（鳥だったら君のところに飛んでいくのに）
例②　I'd have succeeded if you had helped me.（助けてくれたら成功したのに）
例③　I would go for a walk if it should clear up.（晴れたら散歩に行くのに）

CHAPTER 18

Class　　　No.　　　Name　　　Score　／10

CHAPTER 19 接続詞

◎ VOCABULARY CHECK ◎
Arrangement
(1) The traveler walked with a (　　　　　　) on his back.　　　[aabcckkp]
(2) A (　　　　　　) studies matter and energy.　　　[thispicsy]
(3) There was an annoying (　　　　　　) call last night.　　　[knapr]
(4) A semimonthly (　　　　　　) comes out twice a month.　　　[azgmaien]
(5) He received his doctorate from an (　　　　　　) university.　　　[tiredcedac]

PART I　2-33

1. Ⓐ Ⓑ Ⓒ Ⓓ

2. Ⓐ Ⓑ Ⓒ Ⓓ

PART II　2-34

3. Mark your answer on your answer sheet.　　Ⓐ Ⓑ Ⓒ
4. Mark your answer on your answer sheet.　　Ⓐ Ⓑ Ⓒ
5. Mark your answer on your answer sheet.　　Ⓐ Ⓑ Ⓒ
6. Mark your answer on your answer sheet.　　Ⓐ Ⓑ Ⓒ

PART III 📀 2-35

7. How often does the man travel to Boston?
   (A) Once a year.
   (B) Twice a year.
   (C) Once a month.
   (D) Twice a month.

8. How often does the magazine come out?
   (A) Weekly.
   (B) Semiweekly.
   (C) Biannually.
   (D) Semimonthly.

PART IV 📀 2-36

9. What type of school placed the want ad?
   (A) A high school.
   (B) An accredited university.
   (C) A community college.
   (D) An alternative school.

10. What is required for the job?
    (A) Unique personality.
    (B) Bachelor's degree.
    (C) The ability to speak English.
    (D) Interest in psychology.

GRAMMAR POINTER 19　Conjunctions（接続詞）

① 等位接続詞　→　順接＝ and と so ／ 逆接＝ but と yet
② 従属接続詞　→　順接＝ because と as ／ 逆接＝ though と although
③ 接続副詞　　→　順接＝ therefore と accordingly ／ 逆接＝ however

例①　He is kind, so I like him.（彼は優しい。だから彼が好きだ。）
例②　Because he is kind, I like him.（彼は優しいから、彼が好きだ。）
例③　He is kind; therefore, I like him.（彼は優しい。それ故彼が好きだ。）

CHAPTER 19

Class　　　No.　　　Name　　　Score ／10

CHAPTER 20 関係詞

◎ **VOCABULARY CHECK** ◎

Matching

(1) Americans use "(　　　　)," while the British use "zebra crossing."　　・　　・(a) carrier

(2) one fourth or one of four equal parts　　・　　・(b) track

(3) Your train leaves on (　　　　) No. 18.　　・　　・(c) crosswalk

(4) The word "mailman" is now replaced by another gender-free phrase "letter (　　　　)."　　・　　・(d) diploma

(5) a document showing that a person has earned a degree　　・　　・(e) quarter

PART I　　2-37

1.　Ⓐ Ⓑ Ⓒ Ⓓ

2.　Ⓐ Ⓑ Ⓒ Ⓓ

PART II　　2-38

3. Mark your answer on your answer sheet.　Ⓐ Ⓑ Ⓒ
4. Mark your answer on your answer sheet.　Ⓐ Ⓑ Ⓒ
5. Mark your answer on your answer sheet.　Ⓐ Ⓑ Ⓒ
6. Mark your answer on your answer sheet.　Ⓐ Ⓑ Ⓒ

PART III 💿 2-39

7. How long is the flight?
   (A) 6 hours.
   (B) 12 hours.
   (C) 18 hours.
   (D) 24 hours.

8. How long is the track?
   (A) 1 mile.
   (B) 1/2 mile.
   (C) 1/4 mile.
   (D) 3/4 miles.

PART IV 💿 2-40

9. What type of ceremony is described?
   (A) A funeral.
   (B) An athletic meet.
   (C) Graduation.
   (D) Construction.

10. What does the speaker hope the people present at the ceremony have received?
    (A) A carpenter's tools.
    (B) A diploma.
    (C) Construction abilities.
    (D) A desire to work.

GRAMMAR POINTER 20　Relative Clauses（関係詞）

　　　①関係代名詞　→　who, whom, whose, which, that と先行詞を含む what
　　　②関係形容詞　→　which と what のみ［whose は所有格の用法］
　　　③関係副詞　　→　when, where, why［関係副詞 how は常に省略］
例①　John is the man whom she met.（ジョンは彼女が会った男だ）［who も OK］
例②　He's called Zal, which name I'd never heard before.
　　　（彼はザルと呼ばれていたが、そんな名前は初めてだった）
例③　This is the reason why I study it.（私がそれを勉強する理由はこれです）

CHAPTER 20

Class　　　　No.　　　　Name　　　　Score 　/10

TOEIC® PRACTICE TEST

PART I CD 2-41

1. Ⓐ Ⓑ Ⓒ Ⓓ

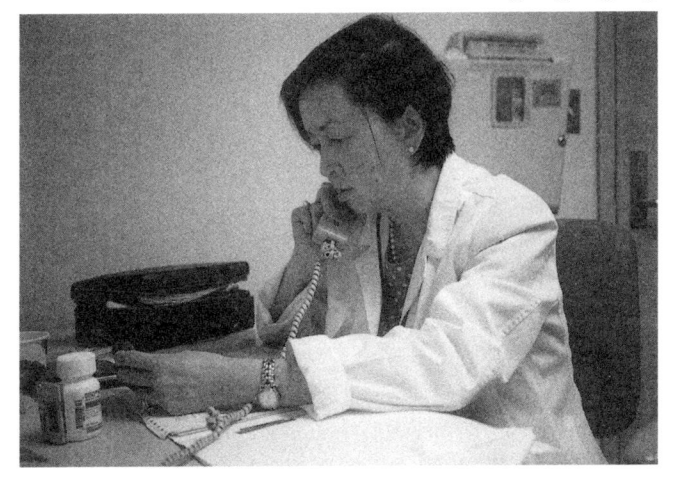

2. Ⓐ Ⓑ Ⓒ Ⓓ

3. Ⓐ Ⓑ Ⓒ Ⓓ

4. Ⓐ Ⓑ Ⓒ Ⓓ

5. Ⓐ Ⓑ Ⓒ Ⓓ

6. Ⓐ Ⓑ Ⓒ Ⓓ

7. Ⓐ Ⓑ Ⓒ Ⓓ

8. Ⓐ Ⓑ Ⓒ Ⓓ

9. Ⓐ Ⓑ Ⓒ Ⓓ

10.   Ⓐ Ⓑ Ⓒ Ⓓ

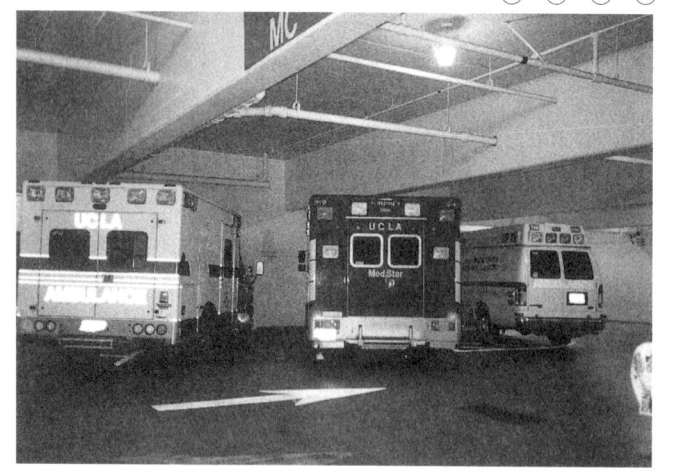

PART II 💿 2-42

11. Mark your answer on your answer sheet.   Ⓐ Ⓑ Ⓒ
12. Mark your answer on your answer sheet.   Ⓐ Ⓑ Ⓒ
13. Mark your answer on your answer sheet.   Ⓐ Ⓑ Ⓒ
14. Mark your answer on your answer sheet.   Ⓐ Ⓑ Ⓒ
15. Mark your answer on your answer sheet.   Ⓐ Ⓑ Ⓒ
16. Mark your answer on your answer sheet.   Ⓐ Ⓑ Ⓒ
17. Mark your answer on your answer sheet.   Ⓐ Ⓑ Ⓒ
18. Mark your answer on your answer sheet.   Ⓐ Ⓑ Ⓒ
19. Mark your answer on your answer sheet.   Ⓐ Ⓑ Ⓒ
20. Mark your answer on your answer sheet.   Ⓐ Ⓑ Ⓒ
21. Mark your answer on your answer sheet.   Ⓐ Ⓑ Ⓒ
22. Mark your answer on your answer sheet.   Ⓐ Ⓑ Ⓒ
23. Mark your answer on your answer sheet.   Ⓐ Ⓑ Ⓒ
24. Mark your answer on your answer sheet.   Ⓐ Ⓑ Ⓒ
25. Mark your answer on your answer sheet.   Ⓐ Ⓑ Ⓒ

PART III 2-43

26. What is the woman's probable occupation?
    (A) Doctor.
    (B) Minister.
    (C) Dentist.
    (D) Lawyer.

27. Where can this conversation probably be heard?
    (A) At a hotel.
    (B) At a travel agency.
    (C) At a bank.
    (D) At an airport.

28. How often is the gym closed?
    (A) Twice a month.
    (B) Once a month.
    (C) Three times a month.
    (D) Four times a month.

29. What does the man mean?
    (A) The movie was good.
    (B) The movie was not boring.
    (C) The movie was boring.
    (D) The movie was interesting.

30. What are the speakers thinking of doing?
    (A) Going to his job.
    (B) Going to a restaurant.
    (C) Eating at home.
    (D) Cooking dinner.

31. What does the man want to watch?
    (A) A play.
    (B) A musical.
    (C) A movie.
    (D) A concert.

32. What are the speakers talking about?
    (A) A television.
    (B) A speaker.
    (C) A table.
    (D) A radio.

33. How much did the man pay?
    (A) 50 dollars.
    (B) 80 dollars.
    (C) 18 dollars.
    (D) 40 dollars.

34. How long was the man awake?
    (A) All day.
    (B) For six hours.
    (C) All night.
    (D) For eight hours.

35. How does Jack feel?
    (A) Very sad.
    (B) Quite hot.
    (C) Pretty happy.
    (D) A little tired.

36. Who took the pictures?
    (A) Lisa.
    (B) Suzy.
    (C) Both of them.
    (D) Dave and Job.

37. What do we learn about the woman?
    (A) She likes doctors.
    (B) She feels better.
    (C) She is afraid of doctors.
    (D) She wants to be a doctor.

38. What does the woman suggest?
    (A) The man should bring a raincoat.
    (B) The man should enjoy the rain.
    (C) The man should bring his umbrella.
    (D) The man should leave his umbrella at home.

39. Which season does the woman think is the best?
    (A) Spring.
    (B) Summer.
    (C) Autumn.
    (D) Winter.

40. Where is the theater located?
    (A) Down in the street.
    (B) In the central part of town.
    (C) Far from the station.
    (D) Near the hotel.

PART IV 2-44

41. What is an alluring aspect of creatine?
    (A) It is stored in our muscles.
    (B) It has recently gained popularity.
    (C) It is a substance found naturally in the body.
    (D) It makes a strong impression.

42. How much creatine is stored in our muscles?
    (A) 90 to 95%
    (B) 85 to 90%
    (C) 41 to 43%
    (D) 19 to 25%

43. What does creatine provide additionally for muscles?
    (A) Protein.
    (B) Sunlight.
    (C) Naturalness.
    (D) Energy.

44. Which kind of subjects are offered at the school?
    (A) Science courses.
    (B) Business courses.
    (C) Art courses.
    (D) Foreign language courses.

45. What is the job placement rate of the college?
    (A) 95%
    (B) 90%
    (C) 85%
    (D) 80%

46. What kind of sale will Bob's Department Store have?
    (A) An annual clearance sale.
    (B) A customer appreciation sale.
    (C) A store-closing sale.
    (D) An end of the year sale.

47. How much will red tag items be discounted?
    (A) 7%
    (B) 15%
    (C) 30%
    (D) 50%

48. How long has Bob's Department Store been open?
    (A) 5 years.
    (B) 7 years.
    (C) 25 years.
    (D) 30 years.

49. What should the caller do to speak to the sales department?
    (A) Stay on the line.
    (B) Hang up and call another number.
    (C) Dial the extension number.
    (D) Wait for the operator.

50. How are calls taken?
    (A) In alphabetical order.
    (B) In the order that they are received.
    (C) They are categorized.
    (D) They are taken by subject.

写真提供
山口　修

Listening Pointer for the TOEIC® Test
基礎力アップTOEIC®テスト リスニング

2003年 1月20日　初版 発行
2019年 3月20日　第10刷 発行
著　者　山口　修
　　　　Tim Guire
発行者　佐野 英一郎
発行所　株式会社 成美堂
　　　　〒101-0052　東京都千代田区神田小川町3-22
　　　　TEL 03-3291-2261　FAX 03-3293-5490
　　　　http://www.seibido.co.jp

印刷・製本　（株）精興社
表紙デザイン　Atelier Z

ISBN 978-4-7919-4574-0　　　　　　　　　　　Printed in Japan

・落丁・乱丁本はお取り替えします。
・本書の無断複写は、著作権上の例外を除き著作権侵害となります。

Chapter 1 Progressive

#	A	B	C	D
1	Ⓐ	Ⓑ	Ⓒ	Ⓓ
2	Ⓐ	Ⓑ	Ⓒ	Ⓓ
3	Ⓐ	Ⓑ	Ⓒ	Ⓓ
4	Ⓐ	Ⓑ	Ⓒ	Ⓓ
5	Ⓐ	Ⓑ	Ⓒ	Ⓓ
6	Ⓐ	Ⓑ	Ⓒ	Ⓓ
7	Ⓐ	Ⓑ	Ⓒ	Ⓓ
8	Ⓐ	Ⓑ	Ⓒ	Ⓓ
9	Ⓐ	Ⓑ	Ⓒ	Ⓓ
10	Ⓐ	Ⓑ	Ⓒ	Ⓓ

Class _____
No _____
Name _____
Score _____ /10

Chapter 2 Perfect

#	A	B	C	D
1	Ⓐ	Ⓑ	Ⓒ	Ⓓ
2	Ⓐ	Ⓑ	Ⓒ	Ⓓ
3	Ⓐ	Ⓑ	Ⓒ	Ⓓ
4	Ⓐ	Ⓑ	Ⓒ	Ⓓ
5	Ⓐ	Ⓑ	Ⓒ	Ⓓ
6	Ⓐ	Ⓑ	Ⓒ	Ⓓ
7	Ⓐ	Ⓑ	Ⓒ	Ⓓ
8	Ⓐ	Ⓑ	Ⓒ	Ⓓ
9	Ⓐ	Ⓑ	Ⓒ	Ⓓ
10	Ⓐ	Ⓑ	Ⓒ	Ⓓ

Class _____
No _____
Name _____
Score _____ /10

Chapter 3 Passive

#	A	B	C	D
1	Ⓐ	Ⓑ	Ⓒ	Ⓓ
2	Ⓐ	Ⓑ	Ⓒ	Ⓓ
3	Ⓐ	Ⓑ	Ⓒ	Ⓓ
4	Ⓐ	Ⓑ	Ⓒ	Ⓓ
5	Ⓐ	Ⓑ	Ⓒ	Ⓓ
6	Ⓐ	Ⓑ	Ⓒ	Ⓓ
7	Ⓐ	Ⓑ	Ⓒ	Ⓓ
8	Ⓐ	Ⓑ	Ⓒ	Ⓓ
9	Ⓐ	Ⓑ	Ⓒ	Ⓓ
10	Ⓐ	Ⓑ	Ⓒ	Ⓓ

Class _____
No _____
Name _____
Score _____ /10

Chapter 4 Present

#	A	B	C	D
1	Ⓐ	Ⓑ	Ⓒ	Ⓓ
2	Ⓐ	Ⓑ	Ⓒ	Ⓓ
3	Ⓐ	Ⓑ	Ⓒ	Ⓓ
4	Ⓐ	Ⓑ	Ⓒ	Ⓓ
5	Ⓐ	Ⓑ	Ⓒ	Ⓓ
6	Ⓐ	Ⓑ	Ⓒ	Ⓓ
7	Ⓐ	Ⓑ	Ⓒ	Ⓓ
8	Ⓐ	Ⓑ	Ⓒ	Ⓓ
9	Ⓐ	Ⓑ	Ⓒ	Ⓓ
10	Ⓐ	Ⓑ	Ⓒ	Ⓓ

Class _____
No _____
Name _____
Score _____ /10

Chapter 5 Past

#	A	B	C	D
1	Ⓐ	Ⓑ	Ⓒ	Ⓓ
2	Ⓐ	Ⓑ	Ⓒ	Ⓓ
3	Ⓐ	Ⓑ	Ⓒ	Ⓓ
4	Ⓐ	Ⓑ	Ⓒ	Ⓓ
5	Ⓐ	Ⓑ	Ⓒ	Ⓓ
6	Ⓐ	Ⓑ	Ⓒ	Ⓓ
7	Ⓐ	Ⓑ	Ⓒ	Ⓓ
8	Ⓐ	Ⓑ	Ⓒ	Ⓓ
9	Ⓐ	Ⓑ	Ⓒ	Ⓓ
10	Ⓐ	Ⓑ	Ⓒ	Ⓓ

Class _____
No _____
Name _____
Score _____ /10

<　キリトリ線　>

Chapter 6 Future

#	A	B	C	D
1	Ⓐ	Ⓑ	Ⓒ	Ⓓ
2	Ⓐ	Ⓑ	Ⓒ	Ⓓ
3	Ⓐ	Ⓑ	Ⓒ	Ⓓ
4	Ⓐ	Ⓑ	Ⓒ	Ⓓ
5	Ⓐ	Ⓑ	Ⓒ	Ⓓ
6	Ⓐ	Ⓑ	Ⓒ	Ⓓ
7	Ⓐ	Ⓑ	Ⓒ	Ⓓ
8	Ⓐ	Ⓑ	Ⓒ	Ⓓ
9	Ⓐ	Ⓑ	Ⓒ	Ⓓ
10	Ⓐ	Ⓑ	Ⓒ	Ⓓ

Class _____
No _____
Name _____
Score _____ /10

Chapter 7 Infinitive

#	A	B	C	D
1	Ⓐ	Ⓑ	Ⓒ	Ⓓ
2	Ⓐ	Ⓑ	Ⓒ	Ⓓ
3	Ⓐ	Ⓑ	Ⓒ	Ⓓ
4	Ⓐ	Ⓑ	Ⓒ	Ⓓ
5	Ⓐ	Ⓑ	Ⓒ	Ⓓ
6	Ⓐ	Ⓑ	Ⓒ	Ⓓ
7	Ⓐ	Ⓑ	Ⓒ	Ⓓ
8	Ⓐ	Ⓑ	Ⓒ	Ⓓ
9	Ⓐ	Ⓑ	Ⓒ	Ⓓ
10	Ⓐ	Ⓑ	Ⓒ	Ⓓ

Class _____
No _____
Name _____
Score _____ /10

Chapter 8 Gerunds

#	A	B	C	D
1	Ⓐ	Ⓑ	Ⓒ	Ⓓ
2	Ⓐ	Ⓑ	Ⓒ	Ⓓ
3	Ⓐ	Ⓑ	Ⓒ	Ⓓ
4	Ⓐ	Ⓑ	Ⓒ	Ⓓ
5	Ⓐ	Ⓑ	Ⓒ	Ⓓ
6	Ⓐ	Ⓑ	Ⓒ	Ⓓ
7	Ⓐ	Ⓑ	Ⓒ	Ⓓ
8	Ⓐ	Ⓑ	Ⓒ	Ⓓ
9	Ⓐ	Ⓑ	Ⓒ	Ⓓ
10	Ⓐ	Ⓑ	Ⓒ	Ⓓ

Class _____
No _____
Name _____
Score _____ /10

Chapter 9 Participles

#	A	B	C	D
1	Ⓐ	Ⓑ	Ⓒ	Ⓓ
2	Ⓐ	Ⓑ	Ⓒ	Ⓓ
3	Ⓐ	Ⓑ	Ⓒ	Ⓓ
4	Ⓐ	Ⓑ	Ⓒ	Ⓓ
5	Ⓐ	Ⓑ	Ⓒ	Ⓓ
6	Ⓐ	Ⓑ	Ⓒ	Ⓓ
7	Ⓐ	Ⓑ	Ⓒ	Ⓓ
8	Ⓐ	Ⓑ	Ⓒ	Ⓓ
9	Ⓐ	Ⓑ	Ⓒ	Ⓓ
10	Ⓐ	Ⓑ	Ⓒ	Ⓓ

Class _____
No _____
Name _____
Score _____ /10

Chapter 10 Prepositions

#	A	B	C	D
1	Ⓐ	Ⓑ	Ⓒ	Ⓓ
2	Ⓐ	Ⓑ	Ⓒ	Ⓓ
3	Ⓐ	Ⓑ	Ⓒ	Ⓓ
4	Ⓐ	Ⓑ	Ⓒ	Ⓓ
5	Ⓐ	Ⓑ	Ⓒ	Ⓓ
6	Ⓐ	Ⓑ	Ⓒ	Ⓓ
7	Ⓐ	Ⓑ	Ⓒ	Ⓓ
8	Ⓐ	Ⓑ	Ⓒ	Ⓓ
9	Ⓐ	Ⓑ	Ⓒ	Ⓓ
10	Ⓐ	Ⓑ	Ⓒ	Ⓓ

Class _____
No _____
Name _____
Score _____ /10

Chapter 11 Adverbs

#				
1	Ⓐ	Ⓑ	Ⓒ	Ⓓ
2	Ⓐ	Ⓑ	Ⓒ	Ⓓ
3	Ⓐ	Ⓑ	Ⓒ	Ⓓ
4	Ⓐ	Ⓑ	Ⓒ	Ⓓ
5	Ⓐ	Ⓑ	Ⓒ	Ⓓ
6	Ⓐ	Ⓑ	Ⓒ	Ⓓ
7	Ⓐ	Ⓑ	Ⓒ	Ⓓ
8	Ⓐ	Ⓑ	Ⓒ	Ⓓ
9	Ⓐ	Ⓑ	Ⓒ	Ⓓ
10	Ⓐ	Ⓑ	Ⓒ	Ⓓ

Class _____

No _____

Name _____

Score _____ /10

Chapter 12 Adjectives

#				
1	Ⓐ	Ⓑ	Ⓒ	Ⓓ
2	Ⓐ	Ⓑ	Ⓒ	Ⓓ
3	Ⓐ	Ⓑ	Ⓒ	Ⓓ
4	Ⓐ	Ⓑ	Ⓒ	Ⓓ
5	Ⓐ	Ⓑ	Ⓒ	Ⓓ
6	Ⓐ	Ⓑ	Ⓒ	Ⓓ
7	Ⓐ	Ⓑ	Ⓒ	Ⓓ
8	Ⓐ	Ⓑ	Ⓒ	Ⓓ
9	Ⓐ	Ⓑ	Ⓒ	Ⓓ
10	Ⓐ	Ⓑ	Ⓒ	Ⓓ

Class _____

No _____

Name _____

Score _____ /10

Chapter 13 Nouns

#				
1	Ⓐ	Ⓑ	Ⓒ	Ⓓ
2	Ⓐ	Ⓑ	Ⓒ	Ⓓ
3	Ⓐ	Ⓑ	Ⓒ	Ⓓ
4	Ⓐ	Ⓑ	Ⓒ	Ⓓ
5	Ⓐ	Ⓑ	Ⓒ	Ⓓ
6	Ⓐ	Ⓑ	Ⓒ	Ⓓ
7	Ⓐ	Ⓑ	Ⓒ	Ⓓ
8	Ⓐ	Ⓑ	Ⓒ	Ⓓ
9	Ⓐ	Ⓑ	Ⓒ	Ⓓ
10	Ⓐ	Ⓑ	Ⓒ	Ⓓ

Class _____

No _____

Name _____

Score _____ /10

Chapter 14 Pronouns

#				
1	Ⓐ	Ⓑ	Ⓒ	Ⓓ
2	Ⓐ	Ⓑ	Ⓒ	Ⓓ
3	Ⓐ	Ⓑ	Ⓒ	Ⓓ
4	Ⓐ	Ⓑ	Ⓒ	Ⓓ
5	Ⓐ	Ⓑ	Ⓒ	Ⓓ
6	Ⓐ	Ⓑ	Ⓒ	Ⓓ
7	Ⓐ	Ⓑ	Ⓒ	Ⓓ
8	Ⓐ	Ⓑ	Ⓒ	Ⓓ
9	Ⓐ	Ⓑ	Ⓒ	Ⓓ
10	Ⓐ	Ⓑ	Ⓒ	Ⓓ

Class _____

No _____

Name _____

Score _____ /10

Chapter 15 Intransitive Verbs

#				
1	Ⓐ	Ⓑ	Ⓒ	Ⓓ
2	Ⓐ	Ⓑ	Ⓒ	Ⓓ
3	Ⓐ	Ⓑ	Ⓒ	Ⓓ
4	Ⓐ	Ⓑ	Ⓒ	Ⓓ
5	Ⓐ	Ⓑ	Ⓒ	Ⓓ
6	Ⓐ	Ⓑ	Ⓒ	Ⓓ
7	Ⓐ	Ⓑ	Ⓒ	Ⓓ
8	Ⓐ	Ⓑ	Ⓒ	Ⓓ
9	Ⓐ	Ⓑ	Ⓒ	Ⓓ
10	Ⓐ	Ⓑ	Ⓒ	Ⓓ

Class _____

No _____

Name _____

Score _____ /10

< - - - キリトリ線 - - - >

Chapter 16 Transitive Verbs

#				
1	Ⓐ	Ⓑ	Ⓒ	Ⓓ
2	Ⓐ	Ⓑ	Ⓒ	Ⓓ
3	Ⓐ	Ⓑ	Ⓒ	Ⓓ
4	Ⓐ	Ⓑ	Ⓒ	Ⓓ
5	Ⓐ	Ⓑ	Ⓒ	Ⓓ
6	Ⓐ	Ⓑ	Ⓒ	Ⓓ
7	Ⓐ	Ⓑ	Ⓒ	Ⓓ
8	Ⓐ	Ⓑ	Ⓒ	Ⓓ
9	Ⓐ	Ⓑ	Ⓒ	Ⓓ
10	Ⓐ	Ⓑ	Ⓒ	Ⓓ

Class _____

No _____

Name _____

Score _____ /10

Chapter 17 Auxiliary Verbs

#				
1	Ⓐ	Ⓑ	Ⓒ	Ⓓ
2	Ⓐ	Ⓑ	Ⓒ	Ⓓ
3	Ⓐ	Ⓑ	Ⓒ	Ⓓ
4	Ⓐ	Ⓑ	Ⓒ	Ⓓ
5	Ⓐ	Ⓑ	Ⓒ	Ⓓ
6	Ⓐ	Ⓑ	Ⓒ	Ⓓ
7	Ⓐ	Ⓑ	Ⓒ	Ⓓ
8	Ⓐ	Ⓑ	Ⓒ	Ⓓ
9	Ⓐ	Ⓑ	Ⓒ	Ⓓ
10	Ⓐ	Ⓑ	Ⓒ	Ⓓ

Class _____

No _____

Name _____

Score _____ /10

Chapter 18 Subjunctive

#				
1	Ⓐ	Ⓑ	Ⓒ	Ⓓ
2	Ⓐ	Ⓑ	Ⓒ	Ⓓ
3	Ⓐ	Ⓑ	Ⓒ	Ⓓ
4	Ⓐ	Ⓑ	Ⓒ	Ⓓ
5	Ⓐ	Ⓑ	Ⓒ	Ⓓ
6	Ⓐ	Ⓑ	Ⓒ	Ⓓ
7	Ⓐ	Ⓑ	Ⓒ	Ⓓ
8	Ⓐ	Ⓑ	Ⓒ	Ⓓ
9	Ⓐ	Ⓑ	Ⓒ	Ⓓ
10	Ⓐ	Ⓑ	Ⓒ	Ⓓ

Class _____

No _____

Name _____

Score _____ /10

Chapter 19 Conjunctions

#				
1	Ⓐ	Ⓑ	Ⓒ	Ⓓ
2	Ⓐ	Ⓑ	Ⓒ	Ⓓ
3	Ⓐ	Ⓑ	Ⓒ	Ⓓ
4	Ⓐ	Ⓑ	Ⓒ	Ⓓ
5	Ⓐ	Ⓑ	Ⓒ	Ⓓ
6	Ⓐ	Ⓑ	Ⓒ	Ⓓ
7	Ⓐ	Ⓑ	Ⓒ	Ⓓ
8	Ⓐ	Ⓑ	Ⓒ	Ⓓ
9	Ⓐ	Ⓑ	Ⓒ	Ⓓ
10	Ⓐ	Ⓑ	Ⓒ	Ⓓ

Class _____

No _____

Name _____

Score _____ /10

Chapter 20 Relative Clauses

#				
1	Ⓐ	Ⓑ	Ⓒ	Ⓓ
2	Ⓐ	Ⓑ	Ⓒ	Ⓓ
3	Ⓐ	Ⓑ	Ⓒ	Ⓓ
4	Ⓐ	Ⓑ	Ⓒ	Ⓓ
5	Ⓐ	Ⓑ	Ⓒ	Ⓓ
6	Ⓐ	Ⓑ	Ⓒ	Ⓓ
7	Ⓐ	Ⓑ	Ⓒ	Ⓓ
8	Ⓐ	Ⓑ	Ⓒ	Ⓓ
9	Ⓐ	Ⓑ	Ⓒ	Ⓓ
10	Ⓐ	Ⓑ	Ⓒ	Ⓓ

Class _____

No _____

Name _____

Score _____ /10

ANSWER SHEET FOR TOEIC® PRACTICE TEST

Class _____ No. _____ Name _____ Score _____ /50

PART I
1. Ⓐ Ⓑ Ⓒ Ⓓ
2. Ⓐ Ⓑ Ⓒ Ⓓ
3. Ⓐ Ⓑ Ⓒ Ⓓ
4. Ⓐ Ⓑ Ⓒ Ⓓ
5. Ⓐ Ⓑ Ⓒ Ⓓ
6. Ⓐ Ⓑ Ⓒ Ⓓ
7. Ⓐ Ⓑ Ⓒ Ⓓ
8. Ⓐ Ⓑ Ⓒ Ⓓ
9. Ⓐ Ⓑ Ⓒ Ⓓ
10. Ⓐ Ⓑ Ⓒ Ⓓ

PART II
11. Ⓐ Ⓑ Ⓒ
12. Ⓐ Ⓑ Ⓒ
13. Ⓐ Ⓑ Ⓒ
14. Ⓐ Ⓑ Ⓒ
15. Ⓐ Ⓑ Ⓒ
16. Ⓐ Ⓑ Ⓒ
17. Ⓐ Ⓑ Ⓒ
18. Ⓐ Ⓑ Ⓒ
19. Ⓐ Ⓑ Ⓒ
20. Ⓐ Ⓑ Ⓒ
21. Ⓐ Ⓑ Ⓒ
22. Ⓐ Ⓑ Ⓒ
23. Ⓐ Ⓑ Ⓒ
24. Ⓐ Ⓑ Ⓒ
25. Ⓐ Ⓑ Ⓒ

PART III
26. Ⓐ Ⓑ Ⓒ Ⓓ
27. Ⓐ Ⓑ Ⓒ Ⓓ
28. Ⓐ Ⓑ Ⓒ Ⓓ
29. Ⓐ Ⓑ Ⓒ Ⓓ
30. Ⓐ Ⓑ Ⓒ Ⓓ
31. Ⓐ Ⓑ Ⓒ Ⓓ
32. Ⓐ Ⓑ Ⓒ Ⓓ
33. Ⓐ Ⓑ Ⓒ Ⓓ
34. Ⓐ Ⓑ Ⓒ Ⓓ
35. Ⓐ Ⓑ Ⓒ Ⓓ
36. Ⓐ Ⓑ Ⓒ Ⓓ
37. Ⓐ Ⓑ Ⓒ Ⓓ
38. Ⓐ Ⓑ Ⓒ Ⓓ
39. Ⓐ Ⓑ Ⓒ Ⓓ
40. Ⓐ Ⓑ Ⓒ Ⓓ

PART IV
41. Ⓐ Ⓑ Ⓒ Ⓓ
42. Ⓐ Ⓑ Ⓒ Ⓓ
43. Ⓐ Ⓑ Ⓒ Ⓓ
44. Ⓐ Ⓑ Ⓒ Ⓓ
45. Ⓐ Ⓑ Ⓒ Ⓓ
46. Ⓐ Ⓑ Ⓒ Ⓓ
47. Ⓐ Ⓑ Ⓒ Ⓓ
48. Ⓐ Ⓑ Ⓒ Ⓓ
49. Ⓐ Ⓑ Ⓒ Ⓓ
50. Ⓐ Ⓑ Ⓒ Ⓓ

‹キリトリ線›